service

VIRTUES OF MY HEART

Written and Illustrated by Melissa López Charepoo

Text and Illustrations
©2020 Melissa López Charepoo

First published 2020. Reprint 2026.

ISBN 978-1-971750-20-0 (paperback)

To all who make the world a better place by serving others.

Have you ever wondered what it means to be of **service** to others?

Service is the act of helping others who are in need without expecting anything in return. It's a virtue, or good quality of our hearts. Doing acts of service makes our hearts joyful and helps us develop many other virtues as well. It can be a complex project or a simple act of kindness.

We can strive to be of service anywhere we are!

At home, I'm always looking for ways to help my family.
We show **love** to our family when we are of service to them.
My favorite act of service at home is to help my mom put away
groceries after going shopping.

How do you show **love** by being of service to your family?

At school, I'm eager to lend a helping hand to my teacher and classmates. We show **kindness** when we help a friend who has a question. One of my favorite acts of service is when we help our teacher organize the classroom after a long day of learning.

How do you show **kindness** by being of service to others at school?

On the playground, I'm always aware of my surroundings.
We show **compassion** to our friends when we watch for their safety.
I always do my best to assist anyone who falls, and if I notice that
my friend is hurt, I immediately ask an adult for help.

How do you show **compassion** by being of service to your friends?

As I learn new things, I realize I have many talents. Talents are special and unique gifts given to each one of us. We show **excellence** when we use our talents to serve others. I have friends who are talented in sports, arts, music, and writing. I love math. It brings joy to my heart when I help a friend understand a math problem.

How do you show **excellence** by using your talents to be of service to others?

In my community, I can find specific needs and think of a plan to be of service. We show **caring** for our neighbors when we help them. We build bonds of **friendship** when we invite others to serve with us. Recently, we realized that the elderly in our community are not able to clean their yards. My friends and I, with the help of our parents, decided to be of service to them.

What needs does your community have? How do you show **caring** for your neighbors? How do you build bonds of **friendship** by being of service together?

As I grow up, I hope that being of service becomes a part of my daily life. We show **commitment** to our community when we choose a career that uses our talents to benefit others. Since I love math, I hope one day to become a scientist and help humankind with new discoveries.

What would you like to be when you grow up?
How would you show **commitment** by doing so?

We can serve our country too. Sometimes natural disasters happen. We show **empathy** when we understand the hardships of others and help our fellow citizens in times of need. Last year a hurricane hit an area close to where we live. My family and I went to help with anything we could.

How do you show **empathy** by serving your country?

As a citizen of the world, I know that it doesn't matter how small my acts of service are; they always make a difference in the world. We foster bonds of **unity** when we think of not only helping our country, but the whole world. We recycle at home to help with the environment, which affects us all. Imagine a world where everyone strives to serve others. It would be a better place!

How do you foster **unity** by doing acts of service locally that help the whole world?

As you can see, we can strive to be of service to others anywhere we are. By being of **service** to others, our hearts develop many virtues, such as love, kindness, compassion, caring, friendship, excellence, commitment, empathy, and unity.

It doesn't matter how big or small an act of **service** is, the result will always be the same. Our hearts will be joyful when we help others without expecting anything in return.

Glossary

Caring – Showing kindness and concern for others

Commitment – Being dedicated to a cause or a person

Compassion – Caring for others

Empathy - The ability to understand and share the feelings of another

Excellence – Being extremely good at something

Friendship – Having a bond of mutual affection with someone

Kindness - The quality of being friendly, generous, and considerate

Love – Deep affection towards someone

Service – The act of helping others without expecting anything in return

Unity – Being part of a whole; togetherness

Virtue – Behavior showing high moral standards; good qualities of our hearts

References:

The Virtues Project Cards

Oxford English Dictionary

Heartfelt thanks to:

My beloved husband Darioush Charepoo for all his support.

Our dearly loved boys for being the inspiration.

Leanna Guillén Mora for helping with proofreading and editing the book.